CRIME AND DETECTION

ORGANIZED CRIME

Crime and Detection series

- Criminal Terminology
- Cyber Crime
- Daily Prison Life
- Death Row and Capital Punishment
- Domestic Crime
- Famous Prisons
- Famous Trials
- Forensic Science
- Government Intelligence Agencies
- Hate Crimes
- The History and Methods of Torture
- The History of Punishment
- International Terrorism
- Major Unsolved Crimes
- Organized Crime
- Protecting Yourself Against Criminals
- Race and Crime
- Serial Murders
- The United States Justice System
- The War Against Drugs

CRIME AND DETECTION

ORGANIZED CRIME

ANDY BLACK

MASON CREST PUBLISHERS
www.masoncrest.com

Mason Crest Publishers, Inc.
370 Reed Road
Broomall, PA 19008
(866) MCP-BOOK (toll free)
www.masoncrest.com

13 12 11 10 09 08 07 06 05   10 9 8 7 6 5 4 3 2

Library of Congress Cataloging-in-Publication Data

Black, J. Anderson.
  Organized crime / Andy Black.
      v. cm. — (Crime and detection)
Includes bibliographical references and index.
Contents: Introduction — The Mafia — Renegades — The Russian Mafiya
— The Triads — The Yakuza.
  ISBN 1-59084-367-3
  1. Organized crime—Juvenile literature. [1. Organized crime. 2. Crime.] I. Title. II. Series.
  HV6441.B56 2003
  364.1'06—dc21

                              2003000486

Editorial and design by
Amber Books Ltd.
Bradley's Close
74–77 White Lion Street
London N1 9PF
www.amberbooks.co.uk

Project Editor: Michael Spilling
Design: Floyd Sayers
Picture Research: Natasha Jones

Printed and bound in Malaysia

Picture credits
Corbis: 38, 50, 54, 57, 61, 78, 81, 82, 85, 89; Mary Evans Picture Library: 64, 80;
The Picture Desk, Kobal Collection: 8, 15, 29, 86; Popperfoto: 19, 25, 27, 30,
33, 34, 39, 41, 42, 43, 55, 63, 67, 69, 70; Topham Picturepoint: 6, 10, 11, 13,
17, 18, 20, 21, 22, 24, 26, 37, 40, 44, 45, 48, 49, 58, 60, 62, 66, 73, 74, 75, 76;
TRH: 46.
Front cover: Corbis (main), Topham Picturepoint (bottom).

CONTENTS

Introduction

From the moment in the Book of Genesis when Cain's envy of his brother Abel erupted into violence, crime has been an inescapable feature of human life. Every society ever known has had its own sense of how things ought to be, its deeply held views on how men and women should behave. Yet in every age there have been individuals ready to break these rules for their own advantage: they must be resisted if the community is to thrive.

This exciting and vividly illustrated new series sets out the history of crime and detection from the earliest times to the present day, from the empires of the ancient world to the towns and cities of the 21st century. From the commandments of the great religions to the theories of modern psychologists, it considers changing attitudes toward offenders and their actions. Contemporary crime is examined in its many different forms: everything from racial hatred to industrial espionage, from serial murder to drug trafficking, from international terrorism to domestic violence.

The series looks, too, at the work of those men and women entrusted with the task of overseeing and maintaining the law, from judges and court officials to police officers and other law enforcement agents. The tools and techniques at their disposal are described and vividly illustrated, and the ethical issues they face concisely and clearly explained.

All in all, the *Crime and Detection* series provides a comprehensive and accessible account of crime and detection, in theory and in practice, past and present.

CHARLIE FULLER

Executive Director, International Association of Undercover Officers

Left: Albert Anastasia, co-founder of Murder Inc. with Benjamin "Bugsy" Siegel, rose through the Mafia ranks to become head of one of the most powerful New York crime families. In 1957, he was gunned down by hit men from the rival Genovese family.

The Mafia

The word "mafia" is often used as a generic term to describe a wide range of criminal organizations that proliferated in the United States during the 20th century. In reality, many legendary gangsters and racketeers, including Al Capone, Bugsy Siegel, Myer Lansky, Johnny Torrio, John Dillinger, "Machine Gun" Kelly, and "Baby Face" Nelson, were never members of the Mafia. Most of them were not even Italian, let alone Sicilian, which was and is a prerequisite for full membership in the organization. True, these men were powerful gangsters in their own right, and some of them worked with and for the Mafia, but they were precluded from membership by accident of birth.

Legend has it that the Mafia was born on the island of Sicily in 1282. At that time, the island had been under the rule of the French for just over 17 years. The Sicilians were used to occupation by foreign powers, having endured 1,500 years of successive conquests. The Phoenicians, Greeks, Romans, Vandals, Ostrogoths, Arabs, Normans, and Germans had all invaded the island and, to the Sicilians, the French were no better and no worse than their predecessors. Then, in 1282, came an incident that changed everything.

In Palermo, Sicily's capital, parishioners of the Church of the Holy Spirit were enjoying their traditional Easter Monday festival when, to their disgust, the ceremony was invaded by a crowd of drunken French sailors. As **vespers** rang out, one of the Frenchmen, Sergeant Pierre Drouet, noticed a young Sicilian woman. He dragged her away from the

Left: Since Mario Puzo wrote *The Godfather* in 1969, the Mafia has been the basis for countless books, motion pictures, and made-for-television movies. The most recent of these is the award-winning television series *The Sopranos*.

congregation and was in the process of raping her when her husband accosted him. With a cry of "Morte alla Francia" (Death to France), he stabbed Drouet to death. A riot ensued, and the Sicilian men massacred every Frenchman at the festival. Within hours, the whole city of Palermo was in revolt and the entire French garrison was butchered. For three days and nights, Palermitans continued their bloody retribution against the French throughout Sicily. The rebellion became known as the Sicilian Vespers. Thousands of French civilians and their families perished, and the

Despite being responsible for countless murders, Al Capone (left) was finally put behind bars by the Treasury Department. Here, he is seen aboard a train with U.S. Marshall H.C. Laubenheimer en route to serving an 11-year prison sentence for tax evasion.

The Mafia was spawned in Sicily. One powerful stronghold for the brotherhood was the small town of Corleone, a name made famous by Mario Puzo in his book *The Godfather*. The "Godfather" in the book was called Vito Corleone.

survivors fled for their lives. France was forced to **cede** control of the island. In the long run, the uprising made little difference. A mere six months later, the king of Aragon invaded Sicily and filled the vacuum left by the French. However, the Sicilians who had participated in the revolt against the French founded a secret society, which they called MAFIA, an acronym for their battle cry, "Morte Alla Francia, Italia Anela" (Death to France, Italy Forever). Seven hundred years later, that society is still very much alive and well, despite many attempts to destroy it.

THE EARLY DAYS

Initially, there was no single Mafia society, but rather scores of separate fraternities scattered around the island. In the province of Palermo, there were the Stoppaglieri and the Fratuzzi, which translates as "little brothers." The province of Messina housed the Beati Paoli, and the Fratellanza (the "brotherhood") controlled central Sicily. While independent of one another, all these fraternities adopted similar rules and codes of conduct. The most important of these was *omerta*, which translates to "conspiracy of silence"; in other words, a vow of absolute secrecy. Betrayal by one member of another, or of the fraternity as a whole, was punishable by death. The supposed aim of the early Mafia was to help the poor against their rich oppressors. In reality, however, their motivation rapidly became somewhat more self-serving. These early Mafia societies financed their operations by being rural gangsters. They robbed and kidnapped landowners for ransom, stole cattle and other livestock, and ransacked orchards and vineyards.

The first written record of the Mafia as it is understood today is found in a report written by Palermo's chief of police, Giuseppe Alongi, in 1886. He described the structure of the organization in considerable detail. He said that for every 10 members, there was a group leader, a *capo di diecina*. This was not only to maintain discipline, but also to ensure that no single member of the Mafia knew the identity of more than a handful of other members and thus was not aware of details of any illegal activities. From Alongi's report, it is clear that the Mafia had long since given up any pretense of being the benefactors of the poor. It had become an out-and-out criminal fraternity, indulging in **extortion**, gambling, prostitution, **loan-sharking**, and a variety of other illegal activities, which would remain their foundation for more than a century.

THE BLACK HAND

The first wave of Sicilians arrived in the United States in the 1840s, and over the next three decades, hundreds of thousands would flee the poverty of Sicily for the so-called "Promised Land." These early immigrants headed, not for New York or Chicago, but for New Orleans. The climate was similar to their native island and, more importantly, there were jobs to be had. By 1890, Sicilians made up more than one-tenth of the population of New Orleans and had risen from the ranks of hired hands to become a major economic force in the city, controlling the markets in fruit, vegetables, fish, and meat. The vast majority of these immigrants were legitimate businessmen who had prospered by ingenuity and hard work, but there was a minority who preyed on them and all the other citizens of New Orleans—the Mafia.

The funeral of New York police lieutenant Joseph Petrosino in 1908. Petrosino waged a one-man battle against the Mafia and was murdered during a visit to Sicily that had been arranged to establish links with the Sicilian police.

INITIATION RITES

In 1886, Commissioner Giuseppe Alongi, Palermo's chief, wrote *La Mafia,* a book in which he described the initiation rites performed by new recruits to the brotherhood. It echoes almost exactly the description of his own initiation rites given by Joseph Valachi to a Senate hearing some 75 years later. Alongi wrote:

"He (the novice) walks into a room and halts in front of a table on which is placed a paper image of a saint. He offers his hand to one of the brotherhood, who draws enough blood to wet the effigy. The novice then swears this oath:

I pledge on my honor to be faithful to the Mafia, as the Mafia is faithful to me. As this saint and few drops of my blood are burned, so will I give my blood for the Mafia, when my ashes and my blood will be returned to their original condition.

The novice then burns the effigy with the flame of a candle. From that moment on, he is a 'made man,' tied indissolubly to the association, and he will be required to carry out the next killing sanctioned by the association."

As the Sicilian-American population increased, it spread from New Orleans to form **ghettos** in New York, Boston, Chicago, and most other major cities, and with these went the Mafia. At first, these unrelated gangs of organized criminals were known not as the Mafia, but as the *La Mano Nera* ("The Black Hand"), and they specialized in extorting law-abiding Sicilians and other Italian immigrants.

The extortion method was crude, but effective. Wealthy businessmen

Wars between rival Mafia families were commonplace as the families struggled for power or control over areas and businesses. Here, we see Michael Corleone—played by Al Pacino—eliminate a rival in the movie *The Godfather*.

would receive an oddly courteous letter demanding money and promising threatening actions if it was not delivered. A prominent Italian resident of Chicago received a typical Black Hand letter in 1902:

Most Gentle Mr. Silvani,

Hoping that the present will not impress you too much, you will be so good as to send me $2,000 if your life is dear to you. So I beg you warmly to put them on the doorstep within four days. But if you do not, I swear in a week's time not even the dust of your family will exist.

With regards, believe me to be your friend.

This and all other "Black Hand" letters were embellished with bloodcurdling illustrations of daggers, skulls, and crossbones, and the inevitable Black Hand symbol. Sometimes, this last symbol was drawn in ink; sometimes, it took the form of an actual palm print. Most recipients of "Black Hand" letters paid up quietly; others refused and suffered terrible consequences for their bravery. Between 1910 and 1912 in Chicago alone,

OMERTA

Since the 18th century, and perhaps earlier, members of the Mafia have been governed by a code of conduct known as *omerta*. This oath of utter secrecy requires that members never, under any circumstances, seek justice through the established authorities and never assist those authorities in the detection of a crime, even when such a crime has been committed against an individual member. However, *omerta* gives the member the right to avenge wrongs committed against himself or any member of his family. Failure to abide by the code was, and still is, punishable by death.

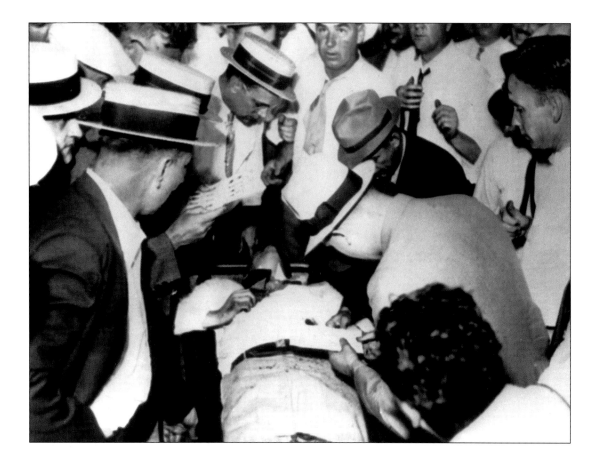

Chicago police forensic experts take the fingerprints of John Dillinger directly after he was killed by FBI marksmen. It was important to identify the body to establish that this was indeed the notorious bank robber who had evaded the police for so long.

Black Handers are credited with having extorted some $500,000 and with committing more than 100 murders.

The "Black Hand" was not a single organization, but a collection of criminals who found it more convenient and effective to hide behind the symbol of this feared and largely mythical society than to operate on a freelance basis.

In 1908, Lieutenant Joseph Petrosino, a New York detective and native of Sicily, launched a one-man campaign against the Black Hand. He had limited, but definite, success, securing several arrests and convictions. In January 1909, he was rewarded for his service by New York Police Commissioner, Theodore Bingham, with an appointment to head up the

ALBERT ANASTASIA

Born in Tropea, Sicily, Albert Anastasia immigrated to New York in 1919 and joined Giuseppe Masseria's family, becoming head executioner. In the 1930s, he and Bugsy Siegel formed "Murder Inc.," the infamous murderer-for-hire business. Over the next 10 years, Anastasia, Siegel, and their associates were credited with more than 1,000 contract killings.

In the late '40s, Anastasia became boss of one of the most powerful New York "families." In October 1957, two gunmen hired by his rival, Carlo Gambino, murdered Anastasia as he sat in a barber's chair in the Park Sheraton Hotel.

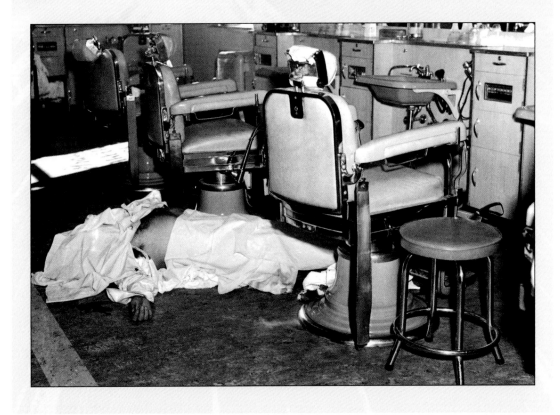

newly formed "Italian Squad." Bingham sent Petrosino to Sicily to establish a relationship with the Sicilian police and to determine what links might exist between the Mafia in Sicily and the Black Hand in the United States.

Arthur Flengheimer, better known as Dutch Schultz, lies dead, slumped over a table in the Newark Palace Chop House in October 1935. He was yet another famous victim of the interfamily warfare that is the hallmark of the Mafia.

The body of Carmine Gelante, godfather of New York's Bonanno family, is carried out of a Brooklyn restaurant after he was assassinated in July 1978. High-profile Mafia murders have usually taken place in public because the godfathers' houses are well protected.

cortege. His family was handsomely compensated with a fund of more than $10,000 and a pension of $1,000 a year, but the Mafia had achieved what they set out to do: they had killed the man they were after. Following Petrosino's murder, American law enforcement agencies lost sight of the Mafia for almost half a century.

THE MODERN MAFIA

Mainly because of the Mafia code of *omerta*, Mafia members who were arrested and convicted steadfastly refused to discuss the organization, let alone name other members, despite threats, coercions, and promises of easier jail sentences. Any such betrayal of the code would have been more than their lives were worth—inside or outside prison. The police and the FBI's reaction to this situation was simply to ignore the situation and resolutely deny that any such criminal organization as the Mafia existed.

In 1957, however, the authorities were finally forced to sit up and pay attention. This was due to the unbelievable tenacity of New York State Police Sergeant, Edgar Croswell. He was convinced of the existence of the Mafia and believed that one of its leaders was a Sicilian named Joseph Barbara. On the surface, Barbara was a well-respected businessman who owned a Canada Dry bottling plant in the small town of Appalachia in upstate New York. Croswell, however, had his doubts. He was convinced that Barbara was dirty and spent 13 years trying to prove his point.

On November 13, 1957, Croswell and his partner were investigating a totally unrelated crime at a motel in Appalachia when they overheard Jo Barbara, Jr., son of the suspected crime boss, making reservations for a "Canada Dry convention" involving 60 people. Curious, Croswell drove out to Barbara's home on the outskirts of town and found several limousines parked in the driveway. Back at the precinct house, he ran the plates on these cars and was hardly surprised when he found that they were registered, not to soft drink salesmen, but to known gangsters from all over the East Coast and Midwest of the United States.

J. Edgar Hoover, the undisputed head of the FBI for many years, refused to acknowledge the existence of the Mafia in America for decades, despite overwhelming evidence to the contrary.

At dawn the following morning, Croswell and a team of detectives returned to Barbara's home to find a dozen more limousines parked there. They were in the process of taking down the license plate numbers when suddenly dozens of sharply dressed men swarmed out of the house and scattered in all directions. Some made for their cars, while others bolted into the woods surrounding the house.

Croswell had taken the precaution of setting up roadblocks around the house, and those who had not fled on foot were taken into custody for questioning. There were some 40 detainees in all—most spoke with Italian accents, and some spoke no English at all. All claimed to have come to visit Joseph Barbara on his birthday. None of them was armed, and, in the eyes of the law, they had done nothing illegal by gathering at Barbara's house.

Joseph Valachi appears before the U.S. Senate Permanent Subcommittee on Investigations in October 1963, breaking *omerta*, his vow of silence to the Mafia. The evidence he presented put countless Mafiosi behind bars.

CARLO GAMBINO

Interfamily rivalries between the various factions of the Mafia meant that being a Mafia boss, or "don," was a precarious business. Perhaps the most enduring and powerful don was Carlo Gambino, head of one of the five New York families. His reign in Brooklyn lasted from 1957 to 1976.

Born in Sicily, Gambino stowed away on a ship and entered the United States illegally in 1921. Over the years, he worked under several of the old-time bosses, such as Joe Maseru, Salvatore Maranzano, and Albert Anastasia, whom he murdered and replaced in 1957. The Gambino family, like all the Mafia families, was involved in gambling, loan-sharking, hijacking, narcotics trafficking, and, most notably, labor racketeering, with total control over the waterfront unions.

In some 50 years of crime, Gambino served only 22 months in prison, from 1936–37. In 1970, the Supreme Court finally indicted Gambino on charges of hijacking, but several heart attacks delayed both his trial or his deportation (on the grounds that he had entered the country illegally). He managed to continue delaying these proceedings for a further seven years before dying of natural causes in 1976.

Italian-born gangster Frank Costello awaits a verdict in a New York courtroom, 1951. For all the muscle involved in organized crime, Frank Costello was the brains that smoothed out the judges, police, and politicians. His contacts in local government, along with his ability to adapt himself to different parts of society, earned him the nickname "Prime Minister."

New York City, 1985: John Gotti, head of the powerful Gambino family, strides confidently in public just weeks before he arranges the gangland killing of rival Paul Castellano.

Genovese, Carlo Gambino, Tommy Lucchese, Joe Magliocco, and Joe Bonanno. Each of these men had a second-in-command, or underboss, and a *consigliore,* or advisor. The underbosses were in charge of a handful of *caporegimes*—captains or lieutenants. They, in turn, were responsible for scores of "soldiers," the rank-and-file members who did most of the dirty work. Valachi claimed that even "soldiers," the lowest in the pecking order, were capable of making millions of dollars a year.

The Mafia as a whole consisted of between 25 and 27 individual families, and the so-called "National Commission" kept them in line. It was a meeting of this commission that Edgar Croswell had stumbled upon six years earlier in Appalachia. Valachi estimated that there were between 3,000 and 5,000 full members of the Mafia ("made men") and at least 10 times that number of associate members, who came from every imaginable ethnic group.

Valachi testified that he had been inducted into *La Cosa Nostra* in 1930 in a ceremony virtually identical to the one described by Palermo Police Commissioner Alongi in 1886. Once inducted, Valachi was assigned to the "family" of Joe Bonanno, who, as Valachi had already testified, was still very much in business. He had later transferred to the Genovese "family."

Valachi went on to give a detailed history of the organization's activities over the past 30 years: the rackets, the murders, the corruption of police and politicians, the interfamily wars—everything. He also identified 131 members of the Genovese "family" and 289 members of the other four families operating in New York at the time of the hearing. Single-handedly, Valachi had blown the Mafia wide open.

Valachi's testimony put J. Edgar Hoover in a somewhat embarrassing position. Having steadfastly denied the existence of the Mafia for 30 years, he was now confronted with a vast array of evidence to the contrary. He admitted having denied the existence of the Mafia, but muttered something about this not being the Mafia, but *La Cosa Nostra,* a different thing altogether. No one was convinced, but no one was about to contradict him.

In the wake of the subcommittee hearing, the FBI and the police made scores of arrests, but these were minor, primarily soldiers and lieutenants. The bosses, the likes of Genovese and Gambino, had long since distanced themselves from the day-to-day criminal activities of their "families." They hid behind legitimate business enterprises, and there was simply no evidence to support Valachi's claims that they were Mafia bosses. In effect, Valachi proved little more than an embarrassment and an inconvenience to them. It was not long before it was business as usual for the Mafia.

The bosses' complacency was misplaced, however, as the FBI poured massive resources and manpower into an effort to destroy the Mafia. Over the next three decades, as more and more Mafiosi turned state's evidence, they made some spectacular arrests and convictions, most recently, the "Teflon Don," John Gotti.

Despite these and other recent successes, the ugly truth is that the power and structure of today's Mafia is very much as it was 40 years ago, when Valachi gave his testimony. The FBI estimates that there are 25 "families" operating in cities across the U.S., but some are now grouped together and controlled by larger "families." For example, the mighty Chicago "Outfit" controls Rockford and Springfield, two Illinois "families," and San Francisco and San Jose are controlled by the Los Angeles "Outfit."

In Valachi's day, the Mafia had its power base in New York and Chicago, but it has long since spread across the country and even abroad. There is a powerful Mafia family operating in Canada, and the Caribbean is riddled with Mafia-controlled banks and casinos. The "families" have interests in all of the world's leading money centers, including London.

Today's Mafia is a highly efficient international conglomerate as rich and powerful as any of the world's major corporations. As Herbie Gross, former front man for the Mafia, put it: "There is the underworld and the overworld, which I call the legal underworld. Where the Mafia uses guns, legitimate business uses lawyers." Today, the Mafia is more dangerous than ever because it has gone "legitimate," with huge business investments and suave, college-educated front men. Today's Mafia has both guns and lawyers.

THE DAPPER DON

With the notable exception of Benjamin "Bugsy" Siegel, American crime bosses traditionally maintained a low profile. Not so the "Dapper Don," John Gotti. Parading himself in his $2,000 suits and sporting a gold Rolex watch, Gotti actively courted publicity and turned himself into a media star. Between 1965 and 1985, Gotti rose from the rank of soldier, specializing in truck hijacking, to head New York's Gambino family. Along the way, he left a trail of bodies, one of whom was Paul Castellano, his predecessor at the helm of the Gambino clan.

Convicting Gotti became an obsession that cost the FBI countless millions of dollars and untold manpower. He escaped so many indictments that his nickname was changed from the "Dapper Don" to the "Teflon Don."

In 1992, however, his luck finally ran out when several members of his "family" turned state's evidence. He was convicted on racketeering charges in Brooklyn's federal court and was sentenced to life in prison without the possibility of parole. Shortly after his conviction, he was diagnosed with throat cancer and was given only a few months to live. True to his name, however, the Teflon Don defied the odds, and lasted another 10 years before he died in June 2002.

Renegades

Organized crime is a global phenomenon. The most notorious criminal fraternities, such as the Mafia, the Triads, and the Yakuza are discussed in other chapters of this book. There are, however, countless other organized criminal gangs operating. These are generally much smaller and less sophisticated, but nonetheless destructive and lethal. Two typical examples of these renegades are the biker gangs and the Yardies.

BIKER GANGS

Twice in his illustrious acting career, Marlon Brando became an icon for organized crime. In 1972, he played Don Vito Corleone in the movie *The Godfather*, which uncovered the previously secret world of the Mafia. Twenty years earlier, sneering over the handlebars of his Harley Davidson in *The Wild One*, he introduced us to the rapidly growing phenomenon of the American biker gangs. It may be unfair to accuse him, or anyone else connected with either movie, of legitimizing organized crime, but they certainly did a lot to add to its mystique, and there is no doubt that post-1953 bikers saw Brando's character as a role model.

Compared with the Mafia or the Triads, biker gangs are a comparatively new phenomenon. They first appeared in the United States in the mid-1940s, shortly after the end of World War II, when veterans returning from the horrors of war found themselves alienated from society and incapable of returning to the nine-to-five world that confronted them. Groups of them took to the road on their motorcycles in search of freedom and adventure. They adopted a confrontational and aggressive attitude, wearing

Left: The archetypal biker, astride his Harley Davidson: leather vest, bare chest, bandana, German storm-trooper style helmet, and the ever-present defiant sneer on his unshaven face. Biker gangs are a relatively new phenomenon, first emerging in the 1940s.

distribution was increased a thousandfold, and for the first time, the FBI and the DEA (Drug Enforcement Administration) were taking them seriously. These agencies made countless arrests of gang members throughout the '70s, but convictions for major crimes were hard to achieve. The bikers' reputation for ruthless **retribution** ensured that no one in their right mind was willing to stand up in court and give evidence against them. In 1976, 16 Angels were convicted on firearms charges and received short jail sentences, but a simultaneous case against Barger and 32 other Angels

Ralph "Sonny" Barger (center front) was head of the Oakland chapter of the Hell's Angels. He is widely credited with transforming biker gangs from antisocial riffraff to a highly organized criminal organization.

SONNY BARGER

Born in Oakland, California, in 1938, Ralph "Sonny" Barger had an early life story that is typical of the vast majority of biker gang members. His father was a violent alcoholic; his mother abandoned him when he was four; he flunked out of school at 14 and drifted into petty crime.

More than anything else, Sonny yearned to belong. This, combined with his passion for motorcycles, attracted him to the Hell's Angels. "I wanted to belong to a group," he said later, "and have a good time with them."

Despite his lack of formal education, Sonny was no fool, and within a year of joining the gang in 1957, he had become its leader and transformed it into a slick criminal organization. He is philosophical about the 13 years he has spent in prison during his 45 years as an Angel: "It's a price you pay for living outside the law...Hell, it could have been a lot worse."

Last released in 1991, he swears he has been straight ever since. Today, aged 63, he still sports his Hell's Angels colors and rides 5,000 miles a month on his $30,000 Harley, a far cry from the $125 machine he rode when he joined the Angels nearly half a century ago.

ONE-PERCENT PATCH

In addition to their own club insignia, or colors, most outlaw gang members wear a patch that reads "1%." The origin of this tradition is well recorded. In 1957, a group of Hell's Angels were riding to an American Motorcycle Association (AMA) rally outside Los Angeles (presumably to cause mayhem). The group crested a hill and ran down and killed an association member. The AMA, anxious not to be associated with the gang and their horrible act, denounced the Hell's Angels and stated that the Angels, Pagans, and other outlaw biker gangs represented only 1 percent of the American motorcycling community. The Angels and their brethren took this as a compliment and immediately adopted their 1 percent badges.

A Hell's Angel biker leans against his Harley Davidson at the "Bulldog Bash" at Long Marston Airfield in Warwickshire, England. The event, which was held in August 1999, attracted more than 40,000 bikers from all over Europe.

for murder, narcotics trafficking, and racketeering collapsed.

The Angels' colorful ferocity and independence caught the imagination of many celebrities. Willie Nelson, Bo Diddley, and Jerry Garcia of the Grateful Dead all liked to hang out with them, and journalist Hunter S. Thompson actually rode with them for a while until he annoyed them and they beat him up.

Behind this appearance of glamor, however, Barger had systematically built a sophisticated criminal empire, which, by the late '70s, was

CANADIAN BIKER GANGS

In May 2002, Maurice "Mom" Boucher, a leader of the Quebec chapter of the Hell's Angels, was convicted of ordering the killing of two prison guards. Quebeckers saw this decision as a huge victory in the province's battle against organized crime.

Behind the trials lies one of North America's longest gang wars. In Eastern Canada, competing gangs of bikers sought to monopolize the local trade in marijuana and cocaine, leading to a bloody turf war that has left 160 dead and even more injured. A police investigation uncovered an operation in Montreal that was processing as much as $1 million (Canadian) of illegal business every year. The violence has often spilled onto the streets of the United States, with killings in Long Island, New York, and shoot-outs in Nevada.

Boucher was successfully prosecuted on the evidence of two former gang members turned informers. As a result, 120 Hell's Angels were arrested, and more than 40 associates of the Hell's Angels pleaded guilty in drug cases. However, despite these successes, the Canadian police acknowledge that Quebec's supply of drugs has not been cut in the least.

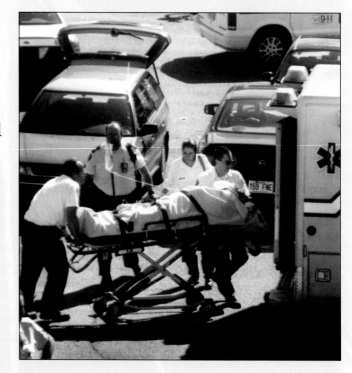

responsible for the distribution of more than 40 percent of all drugs on the West Coast, and up to 25 percent nationally.

The authorities were well aware that Barger was the organizing genius behind the Angels, and they did manage to convict him on a variety of charges ranging from gun possession to tax evasion. In the next three decades, he spent a total of 13 years behind bars. Not that it made a lot of difference: Barger continued to organize the Angels' drug empire from the

Here, 25 members of a Belgian Hell's Angels chapter sit in the Ghent Courthouse, northern Belgium, in November 1999. A group of Belgian Hell's Angels was earlier found guilty of acting as a private militia after a police investigation into motorcycling clubs discovered banned arms.

of Jamaicans seeking legitimate employment came a handful of Yardies. Many of these entered the country illegally, and initially, they were no more than a scattering of petty criminals, usually operating within their own communities. By the 1980s, however, the situation had changed dramatically. The Yardies organized themselves into gangs, and their numbers swelled as the genuine Jamaican-born Yardies were joined by British-born wannabes. They soon established a foothold in the narcotics trade, particularly in the black neighborhoods of London and in other major cities across the country. They specialized in the sale of crack cocaine and gained a reputation for ruthlessness.

Initially, London's Metropolitan Police refused to formally recognize the

The Ingham M11 is one of the weapons of choice of the Yardies. This one was seized by police at the London home of Yardies Richmond Oduku, Desmond Black, and Edwin Appiah, with four other handguns and heroin worth $150,000.

existence of Yardie gangs, much as the FBI had refused to acknowledge the existence of the Mafia in the United States. One of the reasons for the police's reluctance to categorize Yardies in the way it categorized the Mafia or the Triads was that the Yardies lacked a formal structure and were, therefore, extremely difficult to penetrate for intelligence purposes.

A sudden and dramatic increase in murder by firearms (and involving submachine guns) in London during the 1980s, particularly in black neighborhoods, forced the police to take another look at the situation and eventually admit that the Yardies existed. They formed a task force called "Operation Trident," headed by Superintendent Peter Camiletti, whose function it was to investigate the Yardies. The trouble was, the gangs remained as elusive as ever. In 1995, however, two Yardie members, Eaton Green and Elroy Denton, were arrested for a series of violent crimes. Scotland Yard offered them immunity from prosecution  in exchange for information. The two men took their lives in their hands when they went along with the deal, but for the first time, the police had a clear picture of the nature and scale of Yardie crime in Britain.

It emerged that, compared with the Mafia or the Triads, the Yardies were relatively few in number. Green and Denton estimated that the Yardies numbered no more than 200 countrywide, yet insisted that these few members had been responsible for 57 murders between 1986 and 1995, including the cold-blooded killing of Police Constable Patrick Dunne in London in 1993. Authorities today estimate that the membership has risen to more than 500 in the United Kingdom and the death toll to more than 150, almost exclusively black-on-black murders, many within the Yardie gangs.

Retired Detective Chief Superintendent John Jones, who investigated the Yardie scene during the 1990s, confirmed these figures, saying that most of these killings were executed as a "badge of honor...to warn other members that they are not to be messed with."

"The cycle of violence among the Yardies," Jones continued, "is such that a Yardie never stays at the top very long. Their live-for-the-moment philosophy explains why the average life expectancy for a Yardie is 35."

Mark Lambie was leader of the notorious Yardie TMD gang, which controlled London's Blackwater estate. In May 2002 he was convicted on two counts of kidnap and torture and sentenced to 12 years in prison. Lambie had previously been acquitted of the murder of London policeman Keith Blakelock.

Detective Superintendent Peter Caniletti, the officer in charge of London's anti-Yardie task force, displays handguns confiscated during recent Yardie arrests.

YARDIE BRUTALITY

When it comes to outright random brutality, the Yardies are in a class of their own. Nowhere is this better illustrated than in the murder of 24-year-old Mark Burnett in a London nightclub in 1991. He accidentally stepped on the toes of a Yardie gang member, who promptly took out an Uzi submachine gun and blew his brains out.

There were no fewer than 2,000 other partygoers in the club at the time of the shooting. Yet when the police questioned them, 350 claimed to have been in the bathroom, more than 1,000 gave false names and addresses, and of the 270 who were taken in for questioning, not one person saw or heard anything.

THE RUSSIAN *MAFIYA*

Before 1991 and the collapse of Communism in the Soviet Union, the only organized crime in Russia was operated by the government, the civil service, and the law enforcement authorities. It was a regime that was so corrupt, it defies description, based entirely on kickbacks, bribes, and blatant misappropriation of national resources. Generally, individuals or small groups of individuals conducted "civilian" crimes. They operated a black market in cooperation with the corrupt authorities. There was, of course, a certain amount of day-to-day crime, such as robberies, muggings, drug trafficking, and prostitution. But before 1991, this was never truly organized in the style of the American Mafia, the Japanese Yakuza, or the Chinese Triads.

Within months of the introduction of free enterprise, the *mafiya* was born. The Russians eagerly took to organized crime, with many of the first gangs headed by ex-police, KGB, and civil servants. In the summer of 1994, the Russian Ministry of Internal Affairs published a report on organized crime, which President Boris Yeltsin had commissioned the previous year. The report made for grim reading: it estimated that a staggering 25 percent of the Russian gross national income, some 50 trillion rubles, was derived from organized crime. The report went on to state that there were more than 5,000 criminal gangs operating in Russia, comprising a membership of over 100,000. An

Left: Russian soldiers still march proudly through Moscow's Red Square, but since the collapse of Communism in 1991, their presence is little more than window dressing. The real power in the country now lies in a vast network of criminal gangs known as the *mafiya*.

New York's Brighton Beach has become home to many thousands of Russian refugees over the past 40 years. Since 1991, however, it has become a safe haven where members of the Russian *mafiya* may hide.

Before the collapse of Communism in 1991, the United States already had a substantial population of first-generation Russian émigrés, mainly Jews who had managed to obtain exit permits under the old regime. The official figure in the 1970s and 1980s was that 200,000 Soviet citizens immigrated, and the flow of Soviet refugees increased following the enactment of the Lautenberg Amendment in 1989, which allowed 50,000 a year to enter the United States. More than half of these new arrivals settled in the Brighton Beach area of New York, with the remainder favoring California, Washington, Pennsylvania, and New Jersey, all of which had long-established Russian communities.

While the vast majority of these émigrés were law-abiding citizens who integrated themselves into mainstream American society, it is hardly surprising that a certain percentage of these refugees from a totally corrupt society continued their criminal ways. This element, known as *shabaskniki,* were not organized criminals in the true sense of the word, and were mainly involved in swindling the system, an activity that was second nature to them and one that they considered totally normal and acceptable. The *shabaskniki* were regularly arrested and prosecuted for crimes, but American law enforcement agencies did not consider them to be a major threat.

After 1991, all that changed. The *mafiya* arrived en masse and brought with them the sophisticated organizational skills and brutality that they had developed in their homeland. They quickly moved into a range of criminal activities, including extortion, theft, tax fraud, prostitution, and narcotics trafficking. They were smart enough not to take on *La Cosa Nostra* (the American Mafia) on their own turf, so they developed a working relationship with them, paying them a percentage of their profits to be allowed to operate unmolested in certain areas of New York, most notably Brighton Beach. Members of these newly established *mafiya* groups also maintained close contact with their colleagues in Russia, and Russian hit men were often summoned to America to execute contracts.

Russian President Vladimir Putin (left) with his predecessor as Prime Minister, Sergei Stepashin, who is now Chairman of the Douma's Corruption Commission, which is tasked with eliminating corruption in the Russian government.

successor to the KGB), who celebrated the pact by declaring: "Together, we are invincible."

Sadly, this optimism proved to be misplaced. Almost 10 years later, the *mafiya's* presence in the United States continues to grow and become better established and organized. In Russia, their stranglehold on the economy is even more profound.

Some Russian and American experts are complacent. They write off the *mafiya* phenomenon as an inevitable by-product of the early stages of capitalism, suggesting that conditions in Russia today are akin to those in the early American West or that of the "robber-barons" in the East. A leading Russian economist wrote: "The situation in Russia today should not be compared with today's profit-driven American economy, but rather with the rough-and-tumble of America a century ago. The new Russian entrepreneurs should be compared to the robber-barons of those days."

While there may be a grain of truth in this argument, it is generally agreed that the Russian *mafiya* represent something a great deal more sinister and capable than anything witnessed in America under the robber-barons. Senator John Kerry summed up the true scale of the threat the *mafiya* poses when he said to the Senate: "Organized crime is the new Communism, the new monolithic threat."

A Russian police officer detains suspected prostitutes near Moscow, Russia, February 2002. The Russian Moscow regional authorities have started a new campaign to curb organized crime, as high-risk sex practices are a growing cause of what experts say could become an epidemic of AIDS and HIV infections in the area.

THE TRIADS

The most powerful and pervasive criminal brotherhood in the world is not the Mafia, but the Chinese Triad societies. The British government in Hong Kong coined the term "triad" at the beginning of the 20th century to describe an array of Chinese secret societies. It was derived from the triangle symbol these societies adopted to represent the union of heaven, earth, and man. In reality, the Triads predate their 20th-century name by almost two millennia. Chinese secret societies date back to the third century. Initially, they were Masonic-style fraternities, trade guilds, and forums for political dissidence, which incorporated elements of Taoism, Confucianism, Buddhism, and ancestor worship into their elaborate ceremonial rites and imagery.

These secret societies came and went for centuries, but were first consolidated in 1674, when the Manchus, from northern China, captured Peking, overthrowing the reigning Ming Dynasty and replacing it with their own Q'ing Dynasty. For his personal protection, the first Manchu emperor, Kiang His, recruited a monastic order, Siu Lam, whose members were experts in the martial arts. In exchange for their services, these monks were granted some imperial privileges, but, as time passed and they assumed even more power, the emperor perceived the monks themselves as a threat. He dispatched an army to suppress them. Legend has it that only five of the monks escaped the attack, and they founded five secret societies whose sworn aim was to rid China of the Manchus and to restore the Ming Dynasty.

Left: For centuries before becoming purely criminal organizations, Triad gangs were deeply involved in politics. The Boxer Rebellion, which ran from 1896–1900, involved several Triad gangs, including the "Big Swords," the "Red Fists," and the "White Lotus Society."

From their inception in the 17th century, Triads specialized in the martial arts. While many of today's members still practice these disciplines, most prefer to assert their authority with machetes or Uzis.

The family name of the Ming emperors was Hung, and the secret societies adopted the title of the "Hung League." They established their own elaborate initiation ceremonies and secret codes, and all members were trained in the martial arts.

Some members of the Hung League stayed true to the cause and played a significant role in several unsuccessful rebellions against the Manchu. These included the "White Lotus Society rebellion" in Szechwan in the mid-1790s, the "Cudgels" uprising in Kwangsi Province from 1847–50, and "Hung Hsiu Chuan's" rebellion between 1851 and 1865. The Boxer

Rebellion, which ran from 1896–1900, involved the White Lotus Society, along with other Triads, called the "Big Swords" and the "Red Fists." Sun Yat-sen, leader of the 1906 rebellion and the founder of Republican China, was a member of the Hsing Chung society.

However, these political activities were marginal compared with the Triads' increasing involvement in organized crime. From the outset, the majority of Hung League members were apparently more interested in robbing and terrorizing their fellow citizens than they were in ridding the country of the Manchu, and it is these people who were the forefathers of today's Triads.

When Sun Yat-sen was overthrown in 1911, there were no Mings left to restore to power. The Triads' alleged political aspirations finally evaporated.

Fireworks explode over a massive portrait of Sun Yat-sen, leader of the 1906 rebellion and so-called father of modern China. Sun Yat-sen was a fully paid-up member of the Hsing Chung society, China's most powerful Triad of the time.

TRIAD ORGANIZATION

Triad societies have an elaborate hierarchy, with their members organized by rank, and each rank carrying a numerical value. The leader of a Triad, known as a "Dragon Head," carries the rank of "489." Senior officials are rated "438," while rank-and-file members, or "soldiers," hold the rank of "49."

The relationship between individuals is based on ties between Dai-Los (big brothers) and Sai-Los (little brothers). In this system, Sai-Los give loyalty, support, respect, and often money to their Dai-Los in exchange for protection and advice.

However, this did not mark the end of their involvement in Chinese politics. Sun Yat-sen's successor, the warlord Yuan Shikai, was a Triad member. And when the Nationalist government was established in Nanking in 1927, Chiang Kai-shek headed it. He was a known killer and member of the ruthless "Shang Hai Green" society. His *Kuomintang* government was heavily involved in the opium trade and other criminal activities, both during its time in power and after it was forced into exile in Taiwan in 1949.

During Chiang Kai-shek's 20-year period of misrule, the Triads flourished and showed their true colors. Most of the political ambitions gradually dropped away until the Triads were nothing more than an assortment of crime syndicates with elaborately silly initiation rituals.

EXODUS

When Mao Tse-tung's Communist regime took power in 1949, it recognized the Triads for what they were and vowed to crush them. Mao banned opium cultivation, the mainstay of the Triad economy, and imprisoned or executed many Triad members. These measures encouraged

General Chiang Kai-shek (left) and his Nationalist government ruled China from 1927 to 1949, when they were forced to flee to Taiwan. He was a known killer and leading member of the ruthless "Shang Hai Green" society.

Despite the best efforts of the Communist regime, organized crime continues unabated in China.

More than 20,000 drug-related arrests were recorded in the first three months of 2002 alone.

Here, a Chinese policeman supervises the destruction of 1,320 pounds (600 kilos) of drugs.

a mass migration of Triad members to Hong Kong, Macao, and Thailand.

From these relatively safe havens, they established a working relationship with the remnants of Chiang Kai-shek's army, which had been driven into the Burmese highlands, at the heart of the area known as the "Golden Triangle," perhaps the richest opium-growing land in the world. Thus, Chiang's disenfranchised army, under Khun Sa, became the suppliers of opium to the exiled Triads, who in turn refined it into heroin and distributed it around the world.

By the end of the '50s, the Triads not only controlled more than 80 percent of the world's heroin traffic, but they were also responsible for creating totally new markets for their lethal product. This "marketing operation" was seen at its most devastating and destructive during the '60s, when the Triads introduced American soldiers in Vietnam to cut-price heroin as a novelty. Then, these soldiers—now **addicts**—returned to the United States. There, they not only provided the local Triads (now established in every major American city) with a ready market, they also became promoters of heroin. In a short time, there was a massive increase in heroin consumption. No longer was it isolated to the African-American and Chinese ghettos. Now, it had spread to middle-class communities where nothing stronger than marijuana had previously been found. It is to this chain of events that the United States owes today's horrific heroin problem.

While the heroin trade became—and remains—the most potent and destructive of the Triads' activities, it is by no means their only source of income. They are also involved in prostitution, extortion, pornography, and counterfeiting credit cards, CDs, videos, and computer programs. In recent years, they have also gone into the business of human trafficking, smuggling illegal immigrants out of Southeast Asia and into Europe and the United States. This is a highly profitable and particularly nasty business in which poor Chinese pay huge sums of money to be shipped to the West, usually in appalling conditions. Many are arrested on arrival, and scores

Police Superintendent Sue Weatherburn displays two deadly machetes at Charing Cross Police Station, London. They are just a fraction of a cache of lethal weapons that were confiscated during a raid on Chinatown.

in the West. Initially, these societies were "tongs," or trade associations, which had a legitimate function, acting as social clubs for a community alienated from the main body of the population by language and culture. As the Chinese population grew, however, the two biggest tongs, the Hip Sing tong and the On Leong tong, branched out into organized crime. When the first Hong Kong Triads infiltrated the country's Chinatowns in the early 20th century, there was intense rivalry between them and the long-established tongs, a rivalry that frequently ended in bloodshed. By the time the new influx of Triads arrived in 1997, however, the Triads and the tongs had either combined or learned to coexist as they conducted their various trades of extortion, drug trafficking, gambling, prostitution, loan-sharking, kidnapping, and murder.

Unlike their flamboyant counterparts in the Sicilian and Russian mafias, Triad leaders enjoy near-total anonymity, seldom straying beyond the boundaries of their own ethnic communities. And it is these communities that are the principal victims of their criminal activities. There are probably few Chinese restaurateurs, businessmen, or shopkeepers who do not pay protection money to their local Triad gang. They do not complain to the police, mainly out of fear, but also because of the isolated nature of all

In cities such as Hong Kong (pictured), London, San Francisco, and Vancouver, there are few Chinese restaurateurs or shopkeepers that do not pay some kind of protection money to their local Triad gang.

Asian communities, and because they have become accustomed to accepting protection payments as no more than a business expense. This makes it extremely difficult for American law enforcement agencies to assess the exact extent of Triad activity, let alone take effective steps to combat it. What they do know is that while the Triads may operate almost exclusively within America's Chinatowns, the effect of their criminal activities can be felt throughout the country.

For the Triads—and several other organized crime gangs—the traffic in illegal immigrants has become as profitable as narcotics. Here, American immigration officials seize a boat attempting to smuggle about 100 Chinese into California.

HUMAN CARGO

While heroin remains the stock-in-trade of the Triads, human trafficking has become an increasingly important component of their criminal portfolio in the past two decades.

Citizens of China and other parts of Southeast Asia, desperate for a better life in the West, are persuaded by the Triads to purchase "travel packages" costing up to $15,000. These packages include forged documents, undercover travel and legal assistance, and jobs when the purchasers reach their destination. Those who cannot afford to pay cash for the service are offered loans, which they must work off once they reach their destination.

THE TRUTH ABOUT TRAVEL PACKAGES

John Abbot, Director of Britain's National Criminal Intelligence Service, describes the awful truth about these "travel packages":

"Entrants are asked to pay thousands of pounds to be brought to this country, invariably in extremely dangerous conditions— scores have died en route. Upon arrival, they are often held prisoner or forced into bonded labor until their debts to the Triads are repaid. Once in Britain, the women often find themselves forced into prostitution, and the men into low-paid agricultural labor, working for Triad "gangmasters" who supply cheap labor to farmers. While the "gangmasters" receive up to £4 [$6] an hour for hiring them out, the immigrants themselves are lucky to receive £1.20 [$2] an hour for their labor. Consequently, it can take years to pay back the loan advanced by the Triads, who charge them [exorbitant] interest, and those who fall behind with their payments are treated without mercy."

THE YAKUZA

With the possible exception of the Chinese Triads, the oldest criminal fraternity in the world is found in Japan. The Yakuza dates from the early 17th century, and has a tradition of viciousness that matches that of the Mafia, the Triads, or any other criminal organization in the world.

The name "Yakuza" is derived from an ancient Japanese card game called *Oicho-Kabu*. It is similar to blackjack, except that the outcome of *Oicho-Kabu* is determined by the last digit of the total of the three cards held by an individual player. Hence, 9 or 19 would be winning hands; *ya* (8), *ku* (9), and *za* (3), however, add up to 20, and would, therefore, be the worst possible score. Hence "Yakuza" (the combination of the names of these three numbers) has come to mean worthlessness in Japanese society. This does not mean that members consider themselves to be useless, but rather that they are at odds with society; they are the ultimate social misfits.

It is generally agreed that the Yakuza are descended from the *Machi-yakko*, gangs of **itinerant** samurai warriors made unemployed during the peaceful 17th-century Tokugawa era. The *Machi-yakko* (servants of the city) became folk heroes to the ordinary people of Japan, whose rights they defended against the oppressive regime of the **shogun**, much in the fashion of Robin Hood and his Merry Men. Highly romanticized accounts of their heroics on behalf of the downtrodden were recorded in contemporary folktales and plays. It is more likely, however, that the true history of the *Machi-yakko* was somewhat less public-spirited than these tales would have us believe.

Left: The art of tattooing dates back many centuries in Japan. Traditionally it was the preserve of prostitutes, gangsters, and other members of the demimonde. For the Yakuza, elaborate body tattoos became a badge of honor.

The Yakuza claim to descend from the great Japanese fighting warriors, the samurai. In the 17th century, during the peaceful Tokugawa era, the samurai found themselves redundant, and broke up into criminal gangs. It is from these gangs that we find the true origins of the modern Yakuza.

Certainly, there was nothing public-spirited about the true Yakuza, which first emerged during the mid-17th century. The brotherhood at this time was divided into two distinct groups, the *bakuto* (professional gamblers) and the *tekiya* (street peddlers), terms that are used to describe Yakuza members to this day. These loosely knit groups no longer comprised disillusioned samurai, but rather, the poor and landless, delinquents and misfits.

By the end of the 18th century, these isolated gangs of Yakuza had organized themselves into "families," much in the fashion of the Mafia. They adopted the *oyabun/kobun* (father/child) system, a pyramid system of hierarchy that survives to this day. In its simplest sense, the *oyabun* is the "father," providing advice, protection, and help; the *kobun* is the "child," who, in return for this patronage, swears undying loyalty and unquestioning service. Again, the parallel with the Mafia can be seen, with the *oyabun* being the Yakuza equivalent of the Mafia godfather.

Many of the present-day Yakuza traditions were also established during this period. The initiation ceremony was first introduced around 1750. Unlike those of the Mafia or the Triads, this did not involve bloodletting, but rather a highly formal exchange of cups of sake (rice wine) in front of a Shinto altar.

Other ceremonies, such as *Yubitsume*—the enduring custom of finger cutting—were not so civilized, however. In *Yubitsume*, the top joint of the little finger is ceremoniously severed by any *kobun* who has offended his *oyabun*. The *kobun* performs this act of self-mutilation and presents the severed digit to his *oyabun* as a symbol of atonement. Further infractions entail severing the second joint of the little finger or the top section of the next finger.

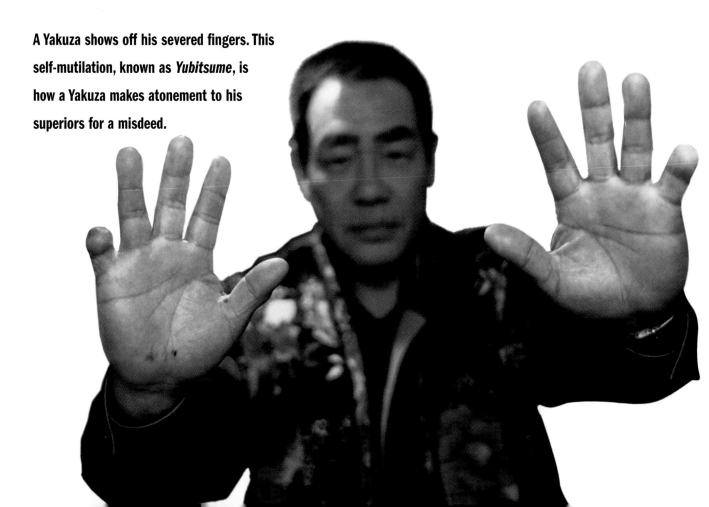

A Yakuza shows off his severed fingers. This self-mutilation, known as *Yubitsume*, is how a Yakuza makes atonement to his superiors for a misdeed.

TATTOOS

Body tattooing is an essential part of Yakuza ritual. Each clan or family has its own badge or emblem, and this is usually the dominant feature of the overall design of the tattoos, together with intricate floral and abstract elements.

For members of the Yakuza, it is a sign of virility, strength, and social anarchy to let oneself be subjected to this long and painful process, with a single back tattoo taking as much as 100 hours to complete.

The tradition of Yakuza tattooing also dates from the mid-18th century. Originally, the *bakuto* (gamblers) tattooed a black ring around the arm of any member who had committed some offense, but later, the Yakuza as a whole adopted this practice, with members covering their entire bodies with elaborate and often beautiful designs.

BIRTH OF THE MODERN YAKUZA

In 1867, with the Meiji Restoration, Japan underwent the first of a series of radical and social changes that would eventually transform the country from a **feudal** state to a modern industrial nation. Political parties and parliament were introduced, along with a powerful national military. The Yakuza were forced to adapt to keep pace with these changes. While gambling and "protection" continued to be the backbone of their business, they took control of several legitimate concerns, most notably the **rickshaw** business.

The Yakuza gradually evolved into its current form during the latter part of the 19th century under *oakums* like Toyama Mitsuru, the son of a samurai, who founded *Genyosha* (Dark Ocean), and his top aide, Ryohei Uchida, who founded the Black Dragons. These and other families began to expand their areas of influence. Like organized criminals in other cultures, they took control of construction, the docks, prostitution, liquor distribution, and entertainment.

The Yakuza also became involved in politics, promoting and financing political candidates who would turn a blind eye to their illegal activities. They were recruited by an assortment of individuals and factions within the government, as well as the opposition, to do their dirty work. In the early part of the 20th century, they were involved with the ultra-nationalists in the assassination of two prime ministers, two finance ministers, and countless other politicians and industrialists.

After Pearl Harbor, the Japanese government was involved in the war, and they no longer had time for internal political struggles; thus, their use for Yakuza came to an abrupt halt. Members of the fraternity soon found themselves either in uniform or in jail. This was not by any means the end of the Yakuza, however, and in 1945, this sleeping giant awoke.

After World War II, American troops occupied Japan, bringing with them food rationing and the inevitable black market that is associated with rationing of any form. A new breed of Yakuza, the *gurentai* (street hustlers), emerged to take control of this racket, and they soon became rich and powerful. They modeled themselves on the Mafia, courtesy of American gangster movies, and wore black suits with white shirts, sunglasses, and crew cuts.

The *gurentai* were even more ruthless and violent than their prewar counterparts. Swords were a thing of the past, and the *gurentai* were armed with automatic weapons. They no longer terrorized only rival gangs, organized labor, and big business, but targeted shopkeepers and small businessmen using extortion and violence. The peace treaty with the Allies had left the Japanese government powerless and the police unarmed. Nothing could be done about the new Yakuza, which continued to flourish in this power vacuum.

Between 1958 and 1963, the number of Yakuza is estimated to have increased by 150 percent to 184,000 members, almost double the number of the Japanese standing army. Just when they seemed unstoppable, however, they started to fight among themselves. There were more than 5,000 different Yakuza "families" around the country, and each was anxious to establish and reinforce its own territory. The result was an outbreak of bloody turf wars, in which countless Yakuza were killed and maimed.

This civil war threatened to undermine the Yakuza's stranglehold on Japan until a peacemaker emerged in the person of Yashio Kodama. Realizing the futility of this internal warfare, Kodama managed to arrange an alliance between the *oyabun* of the two most powerful Yakuza families, Kazuo Taoka of the *Yamaguchi-gumi* family and his former enemy, Hisayuki Machii of the *Tosei-kai*. Given this example, the fighting

Prostitution is widespread and also very public in Japan. It is controlled by the Yakuza, as are drugs, money laundering, smuggling, and countless other illegal activities, all of which help to fund the organization.

gradually stopped, and Kodama was hailed as the Japanese underworld's visionary godfather.

Eventually, the *Yamaguchi-gumi* emerged as the biggest, richest, and most powerful syndicate. At its peak, it controlled more than 2,500 legitimate businesses, along with its gambling and extortion operations, and was turning over almost $500 million a year. Its management structure was said to be the envy of companies like General Motors and DuPont. Kazuo Taoka, the leader of *Yamaguchi-gumi* for 35 years, finally died in 1981. His funeral was a prime example of gangster flamboyance and was attended by members of nearly 200 rival gangs, together with leading Japanese singers, actors, and musicians. While the celebrations were in full swing, however, police launched a raid against the *Yamaguchi-gumi*, arresting more than 900 members and seizing vast stockpiles of illegal goods, including drugs and firearms.

Hollywood has long been happy to use organized crime as a subject matter. Perhaps the most effective and insightful movie about the Yakuza was Ridley Scott's *Black Rain*, starring Michael Douglas.

YASHIO KODAMA

Before World War II, Yakuza powerbroker Yashio Kodama worked as a spy for the Japanese government and was responsible for raising huge sums of money for the war effort. In 1941, at the tender age of 30, he was rewarded for his services with a post as special adviser to the prime minister of Japan and the rank of rear admiral. In 1946, he was arrested by the Allies, along with scores of other government officials, and placed in Sugamo Prison. In 1950, Kodama made a deal with the Americans. In exchange for his freedom, he agreed to work for the G-2 intelligence branch and act as an intermediary between the occupying authorities and the warring Yakuza. Once at liberty, Kodama used his powerful connections to arrange a series of truces between rival families, and in the process, made himself into a multimillionaire.

Kazuo Taoka's widow, Fukimo, assumed control of *Yamaguchi-gumi.* Under her leadership, the family expanded its operations abroad, primarily to the United States and Europe, where their most-profitable fields of activity proved to be narcotics and firearms. They formed working relationships with other overseas criminal organizations, including the Chinese Triads, the Mafia, and the Colombian drug cartels, all of which were already well established in those territories.

In Japan, the Yakuza continued to flourish. Despite their brutality, they still enjoyed the unspoken support of much of the Japanese population, and they also continued to exert considerable political muscle. In fact, when the government finally made membership of the Yakuza illegal in 1992, there was a public outcry. More than 100 lawyers, professors, and Christian ministers petitioned the government on the grounds that the legislation was

RESTORING REPUTATIONS

Since the early '90s, when the Yakuza was officially banned, The New Body Institute, a prosthesis manufacturer in Tokyo, has been doing a roaring trade in fake fingers. These are much in demand, both by reformed Yakuza and those who merely want to conceal their membership. Top-of-the-line fingers, tailor-made from silicone and imported from Britain, can cost upward of $50,000, while off-the-shelf models can be obtained for around one-tenth of that price.

The head of the institute, Ms. Maria Niino, admits: "I have a lot of customers from the underworld. One man's daughter was getting married and he didn't want the in-laws to know that he was a Yakuza. We provided him with a finger for the day."

unconstitutional. The government, however, stood fast, and the Yakuza were forced underground once again.

Far from admitting defeat, the Yakuza took steps to reinvent themselves. They hid their criminal activities behind legal businesses and false corporations and became "legitimate businessmen." Tattoos were covered up, and severed digits, once proudly displayed, were restored by plastic surgeons. They also expanded their overseas operations, most notably in North America. Today, quite apart from the revenue they derive from narcotics, firearms, extortion, and other criminal activities, the Yakuza has in the past decade channeled more than $15 billion into legitimate businesses in the United States (according to FBI estimates). Despite their best efforts, the FBI is virtually powerless to stop this from happening, since money laundering is not a crime in Japan and, on the face of it at least, these investments are completely legal under international law.

Despite the best efforts of the Japanese law enforcement agencies, the Yakuza have continued to flourish. After the government's ban on the organization, its members moved into legitimate businesses and expanded overseas.

GLOSSARY

Addict: someone who is physically or psychologically dependent on a drug

Arms: a means of defending oneself, usually with a weapon

Cede: to yield or grant, typically by treaty

Cortege: a funeral procession

Deportation: the act of returning a person to his or her country of origin

Dissidence: disagreement

Extortion: the act of obtaining money or property from a person using force or intimidation

Feudal: relating to a system of organization in which a lord receives homage and service from vassals

Ghetto: a quarter of a city in which members of a minority group live, especially because of social, legal, or economic pressure

Graft: the acquisition of gain (as money) in dishonest or questionable ways

Hallucination: a belief that one is seeing or hearing something that is not really there

Hallucinogen: a drug that causes hallucinations

Indict: to charge with a crime

Insignia: a distinguishing mark or sign

Itinerant: a person who travels from place to place

Loan-sharking: the practice of loaning money at very high rates of interest

Mafioso: a member of the Mafia

Methamphetamine: also known as "meth" or "speed"; a highly addictive stimulant usually inhaled in the same way as cocaine

Prosthesis: an artificial device to replace a missing part of a body

Racketeering: the act of conducting a fraudulent scheme or activity

Retribution: a punishment

Rickshaw: a small, covered two-wheeled vehicle, usually for one passenger, that is pulled by one man and used originally in Japan

Shogun: one of a line of military governors ruling Japan until the revolution of 1867–1868

Vespers: a service of evening worship

CHRONOLOGY

1282: The term "mafia" is coined in Sicily after the French are expelled from the island. The word is an acronym for "Morte Alla Francia, Italia Anele" ("Death to the French, Italy forever").

1620–30: The first Yakuza gangs appear in Japan.

1674: The Chinese Ming Dynasty is overthrown, and the Triads are born.

1867: With the Meiji Restoration, Japan transforms itself from a feudal society to a modern industrial nation. The Yakuza start to infiltrate industry and politics.

1886: Palermo's chief of police, Giuseppe Alongi, produces the first written record of the Sicilian Mafia's activities.

1906: The first Chinese Republic is established under the leadership of Triad member Sun Yat-sen.

1909: The "Italian Squad" is formed in New York to investigate crime by Italian immigrants. Police Lieutenant Joseph Petrosino travels to Sicily to liaise with local authorities and is promptly assassinated.

1927: Chiang Kai-shek, known killer and Triad member, assumes power in China.

1933: Albert Anastasia and "Bugsy" Siegel form "Murder, Inc."

1945: The birth of the biker gangs.

1947: The first major biker riot in Hollister, California, results in the arrest of 407 gang members.

1949: The Communists, under Mao Tse-tung, gain control of China and vow to purge the country of the Triads. Many gang members flee to Hong Kong, Macao, and northern Thailand.

1957: New York State Police Sergeant Edgar Croswell raids a home in Appalachia and stumbles on a convention of some 60 known gangsters from all over the United States.

1963:   Known gangster Joseph Valachi turns state's evidence. He describes to a Senate commission the structure and personnel of the Mafia.

1980:   Yardie gangs—immigrants from Jamaica—establish themselves in England.

1991:   The collapse of Communism in the Soviet Union spawns the Russian Mafia—the *mafiya*.

1992:   Membership of the Yakuza is officially outlawed.

1993:   The FBI estimates that some 15 *mafiya* families are operating in the United States.

1994:   A report published by the Russian Ministry of Internal Affairs estimates that the *mafiya* controls more than 25 percent of the country's gross national product.

1995:   Authorities in London report that Yardie gangs have been responsible for more than 150 killings.

1998:   An FBI report states that more than 100 Hell's Angels chapters exist worldwide, netting more than $1 billion dollars from drugs, gun running, extortion, and contract killing.

FURTHER INFORMATION

Useful Web Sites

www.americanmafia.com/
www.afpc.org/issues/crime.htm
www.undcp.org/crime_prevention.html
www.gangland.net/russian-mafia.htm
www.geocities.com/napavalley/3143/info.html
www.illuminatedlantern.com/triads/page1.html

Further Reading

Balsamo, William. *Crime Incorporated.* London: True Crime, 1993.

Booth, Martin. *The Dragon Syndicates.* London: Bantam Books, 2000.

Black, J. Anderson. *Organized Crime.* Leicester: Blitz Editions, 1992.

Brashler, William. *The Don.* New York: Harper & Row, 1977.

Freidman, Robert I. *Red Mafiya: How the Russian Mob Has Invaded America.* Boston: Little Brown, 2000.

Lavinge, Yves. *Hell's Angels.* New York: Carol Publishing, 1989.

Messick, Hank. *The Silent Syndicate.* New York: Macmillan, 1967.

Nelli, Humbert. *The Business of Crime.* New York: Oxford University Press, 1976.

Simon, David R. *Tony Soprano's America: The Criminal Side of the American Dream.* Boulder, Colorado: Westview Press, 2002.

About the Author

J. Anderson Black graduated with an arts degree from Edinburgh University. He has been a writer for more than 30 years, and his published work covers a wide range of topics, from art to crime, as well as three novels and 12 screenplays. In the past decade, he has published five books on crime, including *Murder Most Foul* (1992), *Organized Crime* (1993), *Assassination* (1994), and *Crime and Punishment Yearbook* (1998 and 1999). He was also a major contributor to two major crime part-works, *Scandal* and *Real Life Crimes*.

INDEX